John Greenleaf Whittier

A Poetic Offering to John Greenleaf Whittier

John Greenleaf Whittier

A Poetic Offering to John Greenleaf Whittier

ISBN/EAN: 9783743407732

Manufactured in Europe, USA, Canada, Australia, Japa

Cover: Foto ©Thomas Meinert / pixelio.de

Manufactured and distributed by brebook publishing software (www.brebook.com)

John Greenleaf Whittier

A Poetic Offering to John Greenleaf Whittier

A POETIC OFFERING

TO

JOHN GREENLEAF WHITTIER

BY

REV. L. C. McKINSTRY

In Memoriam
Dec. 17, 1807—1834

HAEC OLIM MEMINISSE JUVABIT

HAVERHILL, MASS.
PUBLISHED BY L. C. McKINSTRY
1890

COPYRIGHT, 1890,
BY L. C. MCKINSTRY.

To be credited if quoted.

TO THE PUBLIC.

ALTHOUGH the personal character of the address of this poem may seem to suggest a private correspondence, yet the subjects discussed, and the general esteem with which Mr. Whittier is held, seem to excuse the presentation of it to the public with the presumption that all will join with the author in extending to the venerable poet, greetings and congratulations, and say, —

> Greetings to thee, thou friend of man,
>   Thy life has been a boon to earth;
> Thy years, through all their long-stretched span,
>   Have been a blessing from thy birth.
>
> Ever the world shall bless thy name;
>   Ever, shall men, its accents greet;
> And, through all onward years, thy fame
>   Shall grow and glow, with praise replete.

Our offering is not made with claim of great merit, — only the merit of sincere good will. The public is left to judge of it further. We are decided in our opinions, especially of that old institution of slavery, which has now passed through the furnace-blast for the melting into a better mould, although, from present indications, there is need of a recasting, as it appears that, by some mishap, the melting was not thorough, for there are vestiges of the old form remaining in the hatred of the blacks by the whites of the South.

But we earnestly pray that the country may be spared the ordeal of another blast of the red fires of war, such as we have so recently passed through, and that soon "equal rights" may, as justice dictates, be accorded to all who respect the flag, without regard to color or social condition, and all be treated with respect who are morally respectable.

With this prayer and this hope we send out this book, earnestly desiring that it may aid in some small degree to the promotion of the much-desired end.

L. C. M.

HAVERHILL, MASS.

TO
JOHN GREENLEAF WHITTIER.

DEAR SIR: — To thee my thoughts are turned
    For valid reasons — I remember
That thou and I are, both, concerned
    To note this crispy, bright December.

For, midway 'twixt its outstretched *ends*,
    This *seventeenth*, we, both, were born,
First thou, then I, thus fortune lends
    Its aid to me, some later on.

These birth-events were thus inlaid,
    Mosaics, in this Yankee Land,
Under our Liberty Tree's fair shade,
    Which doth, outspreading, grandly stand.

Our fathers named this, FREEDOM'S OWN,
   And swore to heaven, that their blood
Should freely flow, e'er monarch's throne
   Should here stand, or th' soil be *despot-trod*.

They meant it, too, and did *that* deed,
   Their blood *was* shed, — the soil *is* free,
And despot monarchs well must heed,
   What those brave patriots said should be.

So here, 'neath this wide-spreading Tree,
   We, like the flocks, most peaceful, rest,
And thank our God that we are free,
   And, by His fostering care, are blest.

No place is here for grade or clan,
   For claim of high-blood's *better* state,
But each is, in himself, a man,
   And each, as any other, great.

It is high honor to be born
   Here, any day, in all the year,
But this good *seventeenth's* glad morn,
   To me, is sweetly, doubly dear.

So, double honor, have I, 'neath
  This Nation's Tree on thy birthday,
And, thereby have I that *bequeath*,
  Which gives me honor, every way.

No orient king could e'er bestow
  Such gift, though he had tons of gold,
And I, my birth-right's presage know,
  Though half its privilege can't be told.

It is a gift of right, to be
  All that one can, full-souled, desire,
To be unshackled, always free,
  And feel within heaven's holy fire,

Stirring the manhood's spirit up,
  To deeds of honor, truth, and right;
To drink of learning's crystal cup,
  And ever, for the wronged, to fight.

And not to despots proud, to kneel,
  Nor have their minions kneel to *us*,
But ever with true heart to feel,
  That honor, high, is only thus.

Here wast *thou* born, thy Country told
　　But twenty years,¹ of its life, when
The jewelled doors did back unfold,
　　And ushered *thee* to mortal ken.

Rung out the silvery bells their chime,
　　To sound thy birthday to the spheres,
That all the world might note the time,
　　When Freedom's Friend began his years.

Then, when the first full *twenty-seven*
　　Of thy young manhood's years had flown,
I came, and a good kindly Heaven
　　Gave *me,* *thy* birthday for my own.

Two staid old towns — few miles apart,
　　Fair Haverhill and West Newbury,²
Gave to our heritage the start,
　　The first to thee, the last to me.

The beautiful MORODEMAK,³
　　"*Deep River,*" flowing to the sea,
Or, regurgitate, tide-turned aback,
　　Is silver cord — *our bond to be.*

---

[1] I reckon from ratification of the Constitution, Sept. 17, 1787.
[2] Massachusetts.
[3] The Abenekis Indians say their people named the river, and that this is the original spelling and meaning of Merrimack.

The Town clerks, faithful men, wrote down
    The birth-event, with name and date,
That, henceforth, should each good old town,
    To coming years, the tale relate.

DECEMBER SEVENTEENTH, alike,
    With "*eighteen, seven,*" and, "*thirty-four,*"
That, as the years, time's clock shall strike,
    We'll know our ages, less or more.

Thine are the "MORE" — the "*less*" are mine,
    Less, in more senses, sir, than one;
Less, as to years, are mine than thine,
    And *less*, in deeds of honor done.

But 'tis *my* birthday, all the same,
    And, by it, I my honor wear,
What's "in it," is more bright than name,
    It shines, like *Luna*, clear and fair,

Opaque, but for the Sun's broad light,
    But, shining in his borrowed blaze,
She doth illume the rayless night,
    And men, with pleasure, on her gaze,

Thou art the Sun, — I but the Moon,
  But still I find a light, a ray
Comes to me, as a treasured boon,
  Because I came on thy birthday.

Please, sir, excuse me, though I seem
  To light my taper at thy fire,
And bask me, in its pleasant gleam,
  As thus, to thee, I venture nigher.

Wilt let me, kindly? Then I sit
  With sweet content, down at thy side,
With my poor taper thus a-lit,
  Like one who, thus, for rest has hied.

Thy birthday, mine, most surely is,
  Mine *own* — and why should not, then, I,
Though my flame's fame is "in the *miz*,"[1]
  Sit by thee, in close friendship, nigh?

As thus I sit, and see thee smile,
  By thy consent, it makes me feel,
As I thus, passing hours beguile,
  I do not, of *thine honor*, steal.

---

[1] A little girl who heard read in Genesis "that God made "all that in them is" understood it "in the miz," uncertainty, mist; so I use it.

I sit, and the long vista scan,
    The vista of thy well-spent years,
Thou, noble heart — well-ripened, man,
    Whose birthday mine, so sweetly, cheers.

But thou canst scan far more than I,
    As thou dost, at life's calmest eve,
Look back, with misti-filled, saddened eye,
    To when thou didst thy life receive.

Almost to *then*, — *to* youthful days,
    To home, to parents, days when care
Was not on thee, with torrid rays,
    For boyhood did no burdens bear.

Fresh come those days, more fresh than those
    Which intervene of busier life,
Or later when in calm repose
    Thy mind keeps back from scenes a-rife.

Though long the road thy feet have trod;
    Many life's milestones, as they've passed;
Trusting thy soul a-firm with God,
    Till thou hast come to here at last.

These scenes come not to me — for I
   Thy birthplace home ne'er saw nor knew;
Nor scenes thy boyhood passed hard by,
   Nor what thy hands were fond to do.

But thy mind's eye takes all the scene,
   And mine — the scene of *my* young days,
As flits the light and shade between,
   And leaves it partly in a haze.

I speak *my* birthplace. It had mark
   On "Crane neck road," up toward the *hill*,
And if the shadows come — the dark
   Or light reveals my home there still.

That *is*, to memory — from the place
   The house is gone, and bramble-grown
The grounds — there's but an outline trace,
   Of what I still declare "my own."

My own? although the title-deed
   And claim of legal right has passed,
To other hands, I'll not concede
   My claim to it while life shall last.

For if in mental state alone,
   The cottage, humble home, yet stands,
It is in this full-well my own,
   Although a house not made with hands.

And none can rob me of the power
   Which memory gives, and vision bright,
To keep it as a holy dower,
   In my own heart, by sacred right.

Forty-five feet by thirty-two,
   Was all the land my father owned,
Yet, did the best that he could do,
   And, in that "castle," was enthroned.

It was *my home*, — it is so still,
   As then, though gone the loved ones now,
And tears, my eyes, with sadness fill,
   As, at its shrine, I reverent bow.

Oh! home, sweet home, 'tis true, 'tis true,
   That, humble though the place may be,
Though wander we 'mid scenes all new,
   "No place, like home," we ever see.

No palace built, with turrets grand,
    Nor titled rank, nor coat of arms,
Is like that dearest spot of land,
    To hold the holiest memory-charms.

But honors are not birth-right, no;
    Nor in the blood, nor in the ground;
The well-born man doth, well-sensed, know,
    High worth alone, high place hath found.

There is no caste of rank or clan;
    True manhood, by no "blood-birth," is;
He, who is right, is the *right* man,
    Whate'er his birthplace or his phiz.

So, high or low, the place of birth
    Is nothing, if one, manhood, lack;
Though nameless, 'mong the sons of earth;
    He stands, who has the *stiffest back*

Of moral rectitude, and holds
    His head, with conscious honor, up,
And, in his hands his life controls;
    He may, with kings, right royal, sup.

TRUE HONOR.

Though high-born, one cannot be *wise*,
    If low-born in his soul, he be;
He in his low-born meanness dies;
    There's no high place for such as he.

Name-honor is but dingy rags,
    That dangling hang about a name,
In festoon; musty-odored tags,
    Which smell of antiquated fame.

Man is not great by accident
    Or favored place, or kith or kin,
Tis only by the high intent,
    The purpose strong, that winners win.

Genius is nothing, lying still,
    And accident is fickle, quite,
And 'tis alone by active will,
    And *brain* and *brawn*, one wins the fight.

So one alone, who dignifies
    His name, with manhood's high estate,
Himself, with all the best supplies,
    And is, in truest greatness, great.

You, sir, have never sought for fame,
    Nor I, — we had another way,
Open to all, alike the same,
    And " whosoever will," he may

Walk therein, and be counted wise
    Doing his best ; — with love for all,
Making the highest good his prize ;
    He never shall, who doth thus, fall.

   . . .   .

Now, like the clouds that hurry by,
    Our days tale-told have passed away,
And soon will come the day to die,
    As came our earliest natal day.

We've aged ; thou more, much, than I,
    As thy full years are more than mine,
And mayhap sooner, sir, wilt try
    The dark, death-gateway to divine.

But yet awhile we hope thou 'lt wait,
    And we shall have thee 'mongst us still,
Ere yet shall outward swing that gate,
    For who thy place that time shall fill.

'Tis cheer for us, as though didst stand
  A priest, white-robed, heaven-sent, to bless;
To hallow all our peaceful land,
  While all do thy sweet name confess.

For everywhere with tenderest care
  Men treasure thee, and speak thy worth
As, of a valued fame most rare,
  And thank our God for thy good birth.

It is the praise of men who saw
  Thy love and work, for truth and right,
The spirit of the unwritten law;
  As angel's wing, as pure and white.

Taking the part of those oppressed,
  The outcasts and the lowly ones,
Whom men had cursed, and knew not rest;
  The dark-skinned race of Afric's sons.

Thy pen, which was thy keen-edged sword,
  Flashed, like the lightning when the rod
Cloud-piercing, hears the mighty word,
  Which tells the wrath of the Great God;

Then 'twas as though the thunders pealed,
   As though an angry cyclone roared,
And that iniquity revealed,
   Which stood where-down the torrent poured;

Then 'twas, again, as Moses' rod,
   That opened wide the Red Sea's waves,
Till the oppressed, the dry path trod,
   And oppressors found their watery graves;

Then, like the red, Idumean sword,
   Bathed in the blood of thousands slain;
And, then, like the true prophet's word,
   Which brought the fearful bloody rain.

For, came, at last, that scourge of heaven,
   The war — which felled, beneath its stroke,
The oppressor, curse, concreting seven,
   And thus the cruel bondage broke.

Then, like a spirit sent to break
   The fetters of the crouching slave,
Our Lincoln did the order make
   Which set him free, his rights to save.

SLAVERY SELF-DESTROYING.

That was a day to live to see,
   You saw it, sir, and so did I,
And, ever, shall its memory be,
   Fresh in our souls until we die.

Our good Republic, then, was made
   To tremble 'neath the battle's tread;
And everywhere were men afraid,
   As ran the blood streams, hot and red.

Her life was threatened, as the blast
   Of ruthless war swept o'er her head;
Thank God it did no longer last,
   And Slavery is *forever dead*.

He raised his hand against *her* life,
   The blow fell on his own bad pate,
And in that bitter, vengeful strife,
   He slew himself, in his hot hate.

On us was brought that *civil* war,
   And drenched the land with human gore,
Defiant of our holy law,
   Until we moaned with sorrow, sore.

They said the State had higher rights
    Than the Great Union, and they claimed
That he a patriot is who fights,
    To break the arch by patriots framed.

"State rights," they claimed, forgetting then
    The States in Union bonds were bound;
And one flag floating o'er them, when
    They were not in base treason found,

Meant Union, over the wide world,
    And one good brotherhood, and all,
Where'er our banner is unfurled,
    Must for the Union stand or fall.

It is foul treason to declare
    That States in bond, can separate,
And under some new flag to swear
    The old flag and its stars to hate.

As well may, at the altar, he
    Who, to his bride, his vow declares,
Dare break that vow, and say I'm free; —
    Perjures his soul, he who thus swears.

But Slavery had its stronghold there;
    For *it* men braved themselves to fight,
And rend apart our flag so fair,
    And trample on each sacred right.

It was so strange, when they had stood,
    Our patriot fathers, strong and free,
And fought for what was highest good —
    The blessed boon of liberty,

That these, their sons, should read between
    The lines, another story, see
Another form — of hideous mien,
    The accursed form of Slavery.

It had no place beneath the sun,
    Our flag no shelter to it gave,
And that foul, direful deed was done
    Which made of man a chattel-slave.

Contrary to all the inward sense
    Of right and justice, and the name
Of manhood. It was vain pretence
    To excuse it — and a burning shame.

"Freedom is national," they said.
　"And Slavery sectional"— but how
Could Slavery rear its loathsome head,
　Beneath our Freedom Tree's fair bough.

It was a subterfuge, a fraud,
　To seek to excuse it, and a lie;
And even then they said the Lord
　Did bless it. Oh! how men will try

When choice prefers some favorite thing,
　However bad, to frame excuse;
They will from farthest pole-land bring
　Whatever they can find of use.

So Slavery, here, a place assumed;
　So, Satan-like, it sought to stay;
But, Satan-like, this thing was doomed
　To be accursed and sent away.

Our God had in his Word proclaimed
　"Of one blood, I all men have made:"
And men should thence have been ashamed
　To charge to Him their unhallowed trade:

To say that men could trade in men,
    That blacks were white men's slaves and must
Be held by them, a heaven-wrought plan,
    For masters' service, dust to dust;

That blacks were an inferior race,
    So fitted for the enslaver's chain,
That it were but their proper place
    To work, unpaid for white men's gain.

But He who made the African,
    The Anglo-Saxon, Greek, and Jew,
The Slav, the Moor, or Mongolian,
    Made them all one — old world and new.

And He would not allow that claim
    That one had right, by force to make
A crimeless brother, without blame,
    His slave, — his rights from him to take.

The blue-veined, blue-eyed Anglo-Sax,
    (The cross 'twixt Goth and Anglican),
Could not the negro rightly tax
    To be slave-bound — a fellow-man.

Though white was he, his fellow, black,
   And though he thought white, better done,
Yet that hue which it had caught, back
   Beneath the blazing torrid sun,

Was just as good — once, better far,
   When, in the far-off days, the Slav
Was white, and he who drove the car
   Which slave men drew — did black skin have.

'Twas thus when Israel in the land
   Of Egypt, bowed beneath their load,
Under the hard task-master's hand,
   Spurred on by the sharp stinging goad.

It may not be a pleasant sight
   For blue-blood white-men thus to look
Back, but the claim is surely right,
   As may be learned from history's book.

The change has come, *mirabili*,
   The whites exchanged the place, and lo!
The blacks were slaves, the master he
   Who once the slave's sad lot did know.

How strange but human-like, it is,
    That, give the oppressed one but the power,
And he will put his master-phiz
    Where he can rule, for his brief hour.

But that ne'er justifies the wrong,
    Nor makes a right of what is bad;
The weak o'erpowered by the strong
    Can only make the bad fiends glad.

Thank God the accursed thing has gone
    Into the land of darkest night,
Fled as the darkness at the dawn;
    Fled, fugitive before the right.

Thou, sir, wast sad, and thou didst grieve
    To see the fetters forged so strong;
And much it did thy soul relieve
    To see it go — that fearful wrong.

To see it flee, dismayed away,
    And thenceforth know the slaves were free;
And thou didst hail the gladsome day
    When rang the shout of liberty.

Thou saidst with God, "ALL MEN ARE ONE,"
    One blood, one brawn, one brain, one life;
And when at last the deed was done,
    And Slavery ended in the strife,

Thou didst rejoice, for thou hast seen
    What all thy life was spent for here,
And in the Golden Glory-sheen
    The angels seem to thee most near.

Thy tears have flowed for Slavery's sin,
    But they are dried, and joy is thine,
Because the right did victory win,
    And thy sweet joy alike is mine.

Thy work was Christ-like, when the pen,
    The gyve, the whip, the auction-block
Were slavery's paraphernalia, then
    Thy feet were on the Tarpeian rock.

With thee were men of fervid zeal,
    With righteous indignation fraught,
With hearts as true as flint to steel;
    And everywhere the bright flame caught.

And they swore solemnly to Heaven
    That they would never quit the fight
Until from thence the curse was driven;
    Until the slave should have his right.

And some were mad as fiends in Hell,
    And vowed their curses on the head
Of those who dared the truth to tell,
    And vowed to put them with the dead.

Thou and thy friends who thus did stand
    Wert thus loud cursed, and much oppressed;
But all were dauntless, and at hand
    To stand the fiercest, fiery test;

True to the interests of that hour;
    True to the interests of the slave;
Foes to that fearful demon-power;
    Though threatened with the martyr's grave.

There was LLOYD GARRISON — the man
    Whose heart was to the truth most true;
Who spurned the whole slave-holding clan,
    And did what true men ought to do.

He would, though devils raged, be heard,
    And with a courage grand and bold
Did speak the fearless, unsmoothed word,
    Until his tale of truth was told.

—

I mind me of his paper now.
    The Liberator it, which said,
As lightning speaks from mountain brow,
    With words most unobscurely read, —

"The constitution of these States
    Is covenant with death and hell;"
While it of freedom loudly prates,
    Under its guise slave-holders dwell.

He pictured, too, the fettered slave
    Appealing! — "Am I not a man,
And a brother?" Men did rave
    At such presumption. 'Twas GOD's plan.

The auction-block, the slave-pen too,
    That close friend of the cattle mart,
The master with his whip — so true
    To life — with scorning heart.

John Wesley said — and well said he
   The grand old saint, the holy soul,
"'Tis th' sum of villainies." We see
   That sum to heaven its columns roll.

So thought Lloyd Garrison, and so
   He said, with courage strong and bold;
He would that all the world might know
   That men could not be bought and sold.

He thought — to say, "All men are born free
   And equal," then, some to enslave,
A travesty, a lie, and he
   Said it, with courage cool and brave.

Courage? No hero e'er had more,
   And yet his heart was as a child's;
Warm, tender, gentle to the core;
   And sunny as when Summer smiles.

Few are like him — most cowards are,
   Bold darers, brags with foes not near;
They tell how much to do, they dare;
   But, foemen nigh, they flee with fear.

Not so our Garrison, not he;
    Though not of warrior deeds and blood;
Yet stood so fearless, and to be
    Pelted with rotten eggs and mud.

All for the right and for the slave;
    He dared those foes, *felt* all their ire;
His life's best work he freely gave,
    And burned its holiest altar fire.

A wall of adamant he stood;
    A fortress and a mountain strong;
Great, wise, high-purposed, strong, and good;
    A foe to Slavery's foulest wrong.

His flag, breeze-flung, mast-head was nailed;
    His motto there was blazoned, dread;
And many its grand utterance hailed,
    As they its words most clearly read.

Some cried, Not so. It may be true,
    But say it not, O William, hear;
Else we its utterance may rue,
    For much a bloody war we fear.

And he knew well, *as* well as they,
   Just what it costs to champion right ;
But he his conscience must obey,
   Though he should perish in the fight.

He knew the Man of Calvary died,
   The Christ, the peerless ; why not he
Pour out his blood in crimson tide
   To blot the curse of Slavery ?

Not, with the bloody sword in hand;
   Not, midst the storm of iron-hail ;
Not, midst the soldiers of the land ;
   Not, clad in warrior's coat of mail ;

But, dying as a martyr dies ;
   Struck down by bludgeon, burned with fire,
Amidst the rabble's wildest cries,
   With fagots lit by hatred's ire.

So, die the martyrs for the truth ;
   So, fall the righteous, brave till death ;
So, fall all, in the cruel ruth
   Of Hate-of-right's hot, vengeful breath.

He fought it out upon that line,
   Although it took him many-a-year,
Gained victory — died; and we entwine
   For him this wreath with friendly tear.

We memorize his name, and feel
   That ever it shall be renowned,
And that, time, onward shall reveal
   His head, with fadeless honor, crowned.

WILLIAM LLOYD GARRISON shall be
   Known everywhere, in every land
Where shore is washed by the great sea;
   On Russia's hills or Afric's strand.

CHARLES SUMNER also; he, whose tone
   Was resonant as the clearest bell;
He, who the truth did fearless own,
   And dared it, with his might, to tell.

What though the Oligarch, enthroned,
   Heard all his words, till not one more
Would hear — as thus 'twas freely owned —
   And smote him on the Senate Floor.

So championed Brooks to strike the blow,
   Which should forever silence him,
And thus that noble head laid low,
   With all that chivalry's bad vim.

But " Truth crushed down will rise again,
   The eternal years of God are hers,
While error, wounded, writhes in pain,
   And dies, amid his worshippers."

Thus said the poet — and the soul
   Of truth, these words, metonymic, are,
And through the ages, on they roll,
   Shining like heaven's brightest star.

Our Sumner proved them, for he rose
   A wounded lion, from his mane
Shaking the blood-dew, and his foes
   Must hear his voice of truth again.

He lived to speak, on Senate floor,
   Though suffering pain's hot, blistering feet
As ran they through his nerve-wires, more
   Than Grammograph could e'er repeat.

He lived, pain-suffering, to speak;
   Lived, till the Slavery ghoul had fled;
And though *he*, for that life did seek,
   Lo! Brooks, e'er Sumner died, was dead.

Then Sumner died a martyr's death,
   And everywhere went up a cry,
That *thus* should cease that noble breath;
   That he should thus, by Brooks' hand, die.

But not until he saw the hour
   When he heard Slavery's funeral knell,
Not till the toll, with magic power
   Did its black doom, emphatic, tell.

His brow is laurel-crowned, and light,
   Its radiance sheds about his name;
It glows with beauty, ever bright,
   Shining, through every age of fame.

And men shall speak his priceless worth,
   While Brooks with Arnold shall have place;
Sumner has gained immortal birth,
   While Brooks is ever in disgrace.

To the whole race of kindred men,
    Brooks' name shall be a shameful blot,
Against which ever, will the pen
    Write this — " His memory shall rot." [1]

Not e'en his friends will care to own
    His name; like Benedict Arnold, he
Shall be accursed, wherever known,
    And loaded be, with infamy.

He struck a man on Senate-Floor,
    For words well-spoken in debate,
And covered him with his life-gore,
    And all because of vengeful hate.

    . . .   .

Then there was Henry Wilson. He,
    Who Sumner's colleague was, a man
For Massachusetts' boast, to be
    Forever first, in freedom's van.

How glorious is our Wilson's name,
    Who never faltered from his word!
Dear, ever will he be to fame,
    His voice, like lion's roar was heard.

[1] Prov. x. 7.

Heard, for the bondmen, the oppressed;
   Heard, for the right against the wrong;
Heard, for the poor and the distressed;
   Heard, for the weak against the strong.

Oh Wilson! name, though borrowed, first,
   The poor boy's waif-name, now it stands,
A name phenomenal; like a sunburst
   It glows and gleams through far-off lands.

. . .   .

There was our Phillips, too, whose voice
   Was clear as silver trumpet-blast;
The pure, unsullied, who of choice
   Did stand alone, from first to last.

How dared he every rabble throng,
   In Faneuil Hall and everywhere,
Fighting his battles well and long,
   Till worn at last, with pain and care.

He championed right when in the dust
   It lay, down-trodden, bruised, and torn,
Because he felt its cause was just,
   The-while with gyves its limbs were worn.

He raised it, ragged and besmeared ;
   Then stood beside it, like a king,
While angry foes with eyes a-bleared,
   Did, at him, dirtiest missiles fling.

I see him now, his eyes a-gleam ;
   His voice, though calm, with force alive,
Pouring invective like a stream
   Red-hot, till even fiends did writhe.

How sharp his tongue, yet smooth as oil ;
   How calm his words, yet full of fire,
Sarcasm, irony ; to foil
   The venomed Serpent's fiendish ire.

He saw, at last, the victory won ;
   He saw the sullen foe shrink back ;
He saw, when all the work was done ;
   He saw, with courage near a-lack.

Thank God he lived, and saw the day
   When he could speak, and cheer on cheer
Greeted his words. He won his way,
   And now his name is, henceforth, dear.

We'll build for him memorial, grand;
   A HALL, to truth and right; his name
Shall grace it, it shall stand
   The glorious tribute to his fame.

What a grand Galaxy were they,
   Those patriot men, who, side by side,
Stood in the thickest of the fray,
   And in the fight, won, e'er they died.

Never, one swerved from path of right,
   Whatever threatened him. They knew
The fiery perils of the fight,
   But, stood, to each, and honor, true.

   . . .   .

We mention, now, a *woman's* name,
   Well-known, where'er men, hurrying, go;
World-wide, with ever growing fame;
   That woman — HARRIET BEECHER STOWE.

What work her trenchant pen did do,
   When she, her tale of Slavery, told,
Laid bare its character, — So true
   A tale will ne'er come stale and old.

Full-humored it, with wit of those,
    Who bore, so well, their toilsome lot;
Full-burdened with *their* deep-throed woes,
    Whose human sense, masters forgot.

No phase of life but she portrayed;
    No character but she described;
And well she Uncle Tom arrayed,
    In Christian honor, till he died.

Then, in full-contrast, like a pearl,
    Set in the polished, native jet,
Was EVA, — pure-souled, loving girl, —
    Of UNCLE TOM, the Teacher-Pet.

To tell him, better, of the home
    The Bible Home, her faith-clear eyes
Saw, as she read, whose wall and dome
    Were, to her, hopeful, glad surprise.

Then, when at length poor Tom laid down
    To die, whipped, like a dog, to death,
Was, for her words, the martyr's crown
    Brighter — as breathed he his last breath.

Oh, she who told that tale, did do
    What, else, forever, were undone,
What, if not done, we still might view
    That foul Accursion, 'neath the Sun.

Deep, laid she, her dynamite train,
    Beneath the structure Slavery raised,
We *heard,* we *felt,* when o'er the main
    Came the explosion — God be praised,

That thus a woman's hand had skill
    To touch the button, and we know,
That it was, by Heaven's good, high will,
    She thus did slavery overthrow.

Aged now and feeble, still she lives,
    That woman, waiting at her Rest;
Enjoying what her prestige gives;
    A woman, ranked among the best,

Happy, while in her evening hour,
    She feels no care, and knows no foe,
As, in her quiet, rose-bloomed bower,
    She does, the well-done-plaudit, know.

A pleasant evening to her, now;
    Her laurels never hence will fade;
Calmness rests sweetly on her brow;
    Her credit-score is summed, and made.

She waits content, and, if it be
    That light goes out, e'er day shall close,
Then, still, her honor shines, and she
    Shall, only fade, as fades the rose,

Her perfume lingering in the tale
    She told, in all its classic phrase;
When she lies down in death's still vale,
    She shall be, of all tongues, the praise.

. . .   .

These were *thy* friends, and thou among
    Them, in the Galaxy, hast place;
Named in all lands by every tongue,
    Crowned with high honor, truth, and grace.

And, as thou sittest down serene,
    In life's calm, placid, twilight eve,
Watching the shadows intervene,
    Till thou, thy summons shalt receive,

Thou seest all the record-page
   Of this great history of the fight,
Of which, henceforth, the wisest sage,
   Shall speak, when championing the right.

Oh, blessed art thou, friend of man,
   Whose pen was like a shaft of light,
Which through the darkness sped, to span
   The space of Slavery's fearful night.

From thee *I* learned of Liberty,
   The goddess of the fairest mold,
And in her face I learned to see,
   Slavery condemned, in line-signs bold.

From thee, I learned to love the slave,
   And pray to God to set him free,
His friend, the true one, strong, and bold,
   I saw thee, Whittier, to be.

I saw thy work, I saw the power,
   That held the slave, that bade him toil
Unpaid, through many a weary hour,
   Until my blood, did, heated, boil.

WORK: REST: GIFTS.

Oh, 'tis not strange, that now, the deed
    Is done, which gave him liberty,
And he is, from his bondage freed,
    Men pay their honors unto thee,

And bring thee gifts, upon the day,
    Th' anniversary of thy birth,
Showering their blessings on thy way,
    As on the chosen of the earth.

Oh! what a work thy hands have wrought;
    Oh! what a history, grand, is thine;
Oh! what a boon have I, thus caught
    In thy birthday, to make it mine.

Thy work is nearly done, and thou
    Mayest now be longing for thy rest,
As, on thy aged, white-haired brow,
    Flashes the radiance of the blest.

But I, perchance, may still work on,
    With head, with all my earnest heart;
When thou art, to the death-shades, gone,
    From life, and all its scenes, apart.

Not I alone; all men may find
    The world work-full, for those in need
Of helpful hands, and true words, kind;
    Giving to, burdened sufferers, heed.

The sufferers, crying in the night;
    The weary, with their burdening cares;
The blinded, crying for the light;
    The helpless, crying for our prayers.

And who, for right's sake toils, shall find
    What will make hearts of flesh, so feel
The burdens which the cruel bind,
    That they, as with an arm of steel,

Shall wrench the bands asunder, though
    Bound by a welding furnace-blast;
Breaking them, as a thread of tow;
    Them, into Ocean's depths, to cast.

And, thus, new fields before us lie,
    Where foes in legions strong are massed;
Who, or *we*, must, in conflict, die,
    And, on they come, in fury fast.

THE FREEDMEN'S SOCIAL STATUS. 45

The freedmen's battles are not fought,
    Although full citizens they be,
Our equals; though so much is wrought,
    And they are now, forever free.

And, though they in full manhood stand,
    Equal with all, before the law,
Their highest privilege to command,
    With rights they bravely battled for.

Their social status now is made
    The question, and the strife is on,
The war of races. Sore afraid
    Are many, sitting down forlorn,

Or, fleeing to some other clime,
    To far Liberia, or a state,
Where they may dwell, in place and time
    Apart from others' blue-blood, hate.

What does it mean? Where is the sense
    Of men who once *must* have them near,
As toiling slaves? What the pretence
    They have for this, is not quite clear.

It is a shame — a *burning* shame,
   That color-lines should, thus, be drawn;
That white-skins should the black ones blame,
   As though themselves were better born.

What had they of their *white* to say?
   What could they, with their color do?
Sometimes, to mix it in the way,
   To whiten out the black skin's hue.

Then, for the stains of black, still there,
   Condemn their own to lowest grade,
Though they have in it their full share,
   And have, their low-born lust, betrayed.

'Tis a dishonor, thus to shun,
   Their own blood — their own kith and kin;
Those rivulets that, 'neath black skins run,
   Have strains, too much of theirs, therein.

Yet in the cars these skins can't ride;
   Because the color is there still;
Nor in a city-home, abide,
   Although they have the *cash* and *will*.

Nor can black children go to school,
  Where white men's children, high-toned, go,
Although they, well-trained, keep each rule,
  And quick adeptness, clearly show.

Thus 'tis, and law men nullify,
  Which gives, to all, their equal dower,
Of Freedom-rights; — they thus defy,
  The Great Republic's strong-armed power.

But they must know they cannot do,
  Such hateful deeds, and hold their place;
Our Government, forever true,
  Must stand by that poor, out-cast race.

The Independent States may claim,
  The right to make their own race-laws,
But, over all is that *one name*,
  THE UNITED STATES, to bid them pause;

To show them that they cannot do,
  Whate'er, *as* States, they choose, and be
Allowed to put their base schemes through,
  And not a Federal signal see,

To warn them that our government,
   Still holds, its sway, and can, again,
Show 'tis her high and right intent,
   All lawless measures to restrain.

She'll do it, too, and law shall be,
   Through every State, by right sustained,
Though, once, again, unwilled, we see,
   The dreadful storm of leaden rain.

The boys of *sixty-one*, still live,
   And have begotten many a son,
And they are ready, and will give
   Their lives, that truth's rights may be won.

The G. A. R.'s and S. of V.'s,
   Are like a bond of glittering gold,
Fire-tried, and each, with keen eye sees
   Still, the star-striped flag's bright folds.

And ballots, or the bullets, must
   Settle the question through the land,
For this grand cause, so good and just;
   Cause, held in God's almighty hand.

THE BALLOT, OR THE BULLET.

'Tis ballots first — the freemen's will
    Is in them, as, upon the sod,
The snow-flakes, falling, white and still,
    Are the winged messengers of God.

And all, their ballot-rights, must have,
    Whate'er their race or color be;
The black or white, the celt or slav,
    Must have the ballot's ministry.

Or else the *bullet* comes, to show
    The nullifier cannot rule,
But must the fearful ordeal know,
    And learn in war's hot-tempered school,

The lessons, which are learned alone,
    By those who elsewhere will not learn;
Who will not, truth's sweet teachings own,
    But all its mandates, madly spurn.

And, if the Southron would have peace,
    And keep the hot-sped bullet back,
Then he, his tyranny, must cease,
    And cease to persecute the black.

He must allow each man his place,
    Though black as night, his color be,
And cease, because of dark-hued face,
    To brand a man with infamy.

At school, at church, on cars, he must
    Give place to him, as other men,
It is his right, his cause is just,
    And all the world should say *Amen.*

And woe to him, who dares to try,
    To crowd this brother-man, aside,
Or crush him down; the law is nigh,
    And such, its sentence must abide.

For, only, when its claims are known,
    And its behests are recognized,
Do men their proper standing own,
    Or are their rights in due sense, prized.

'Tis thus the colored man has place,
    Has equal rights with white men; he
Of truest manhood every trace
    Shows, though 'tis set in ebony.

THE MONGOLIAN.

And still there is another race,
   The almond-eyed Mongolians. They
Cannot here, have a home-place,
   But must, with haste, hie them away

From this fair land, where Freedom's bird
   Sits, meditate; or spreads his wings
Sun-eying, till his scream is heard
   Where th' Sun, his light o'er mount-peak flings.

Oh, eagle! proud bird of our land!
   What think ye, as ye scream on high,
Of this, our hateful, base command,
   That Chinamen must not come nigh?

'Tis true we've pledged, our crust to share,
   With who-so, ship from far-land brings;
'Tis true there room is, everywhere,
   Where sweet contentment sits and sings.

But *Chinaman*, though he, quietly
   Comes here, to live, and earn his bread,
Must never dare here-at to stay,
   Else goes his queue, perhaps,—his head.

An alien he, to be cast out,
    To have no portion in this land;
His Queue-Clan we must quickly rout,
    We must not give him friendly hand.

He works too cheaply, eats his "rice,"
    He *washee Melican* man's shirts;
And though he does them extra nice,
    And equal to the best experts,

He must not stay, he can't abide
    Within our Domain, though it be
A place where one may safely hide
    From poverty, beneath our Tree.

He, "Heathen Chinee," at our door
    Stands, asking us to give him light;
Seeking to learn, that he the more
    May know, and do more fully, right.

We send our Missionaries there,
    To China, costing thousands, so
The Chinamen, with closest care
    The Christ, may, through the gospel, know.

But when they come to us, straightway
  We say, "No. John, no *heree* come;
You must not *learnee* here to pray;
  Go home, and pray to idols dumb."

Oh, is this where our fathers died?
  Is this the land of Washington?
Is this our Pilgrim Fathers' pride?
  This land, where such base thing is done?

Yes, shame to own it, loath are we,
  But 'tis the land, the very same;
Alas! perhaps it yet may be,
  That 'tis the land in but its name.

'Tis not for foreign paupers, no;
  Nor for the banished criminals;
Those Countries to their poor ones owe
  Support, and to their felons *cells*.

For every vicious criminal
  Who here is found, a banished fiend,
Turns happiest place to misriest hell,
  And he cannot be, here, convened.

Our Freedom, never, senseless, means
    License, nor lazy indolence;
Nor, that the man who, sleeping, dreams
    Of luck, shall e'er get rich, by chance.

It never means that one is great
    Because he has his pile of dust;
Nor a long-genealogued estate;
    Nor coat-of-arm, o'er-spread with rust.

It means not, that a place, has, here
    The Anarchist, who is the foe
Of Governments, to fill with fear
    Those, who their lawlessness well know.

But 'tis the loyal man who may
    Come here to live, to work, to vote;
To be a true man every way;
    Whether unknown, or, one of note.

All honest men, whate'er their creed,
    Who come respecting our good flag,
Who of our comforts stand in need,
    Who will not hoist a rebel rag,

They may come here, to till the soil,
    For brain-work, or, with willing hands,
In shops, or elsewhere, by their toil
    To help our best-of-all-earth's-lands.

No matter from what land they come;
    No matter what their tongue may be;
No matter what the rounded sum
    Of their vast multitudes, we see.

They have a right here, if they will
    Keep our just laws, with loyal heart;
Each one his place, best fit, to fill;
    To do his honest, manly part.

To make our land a place of thrift,
    Of busy industry and life;
To keep a-back the floating drift
    Of evil, gendering bloody strife.

And in his right, must each have guard,
    To be a man — with life, and right
To fix his price for his reward
    Of labor, whether day or night.

And all because our government,
　　Firmly on its foundations, stands,
And shows that 'tis its wise intent
　　To well-enforce its law's demands.

The rights of all to fully shield,
　　The while unforfeit they shall be;
And its strong power, to, wisely, wield
　　'Gainst Oligarch and anarchy.

So all men equal-born, may find
　　They, equal *are*, before the law,
And that the government is kind,
　　Though vested with the proper awe,

And swiftly seizes those who dare
　　The law's behests to disobey,
Forgetful that the lawless bear
　　Its equal, penal-curse, alway.

It can no combined force protect,
　　No Clan-na-Gael — in our land;
And all who are by us "suspect,"
　　Must, at our court's-tribunal, stand.

NO DRUNKARD-MAKERS ALLOWED. 57

And every law must so be made
    That right shall, vested, in it be,
And none by fraud be e'er betrayed,
    And none who should be bound, go free,

And none allowed, though he might pay
    High License for especial right,
To hurt his neighbor any way,
    In purse or manhood, day or night,

Nor drunkard-makers be allowed
    To drunkards make at any price,
No more than he, who in a crowd
    Picks pockets, by his cool device.

Then, can the laborer to his toil
    Off, whistling, go, and he of means
Live happily — all by fruitful soil
    Be well-fed, by what he well, deems,

His best pursuit, — his highest aim,
    To feel that he is, all, a man,
And every other, is the same,
    Who does the best a mortal can.

The government can then control
　　All our great interests, and no more
Shall corporations, without soul,
　　Grind down the faces of the poor,

And one may, any one employ,
　　Whom he shall choose, at proper wage,
And one may, his high right enjoy,
　　To work, wherever he engage.

And labor be the capital,
　　And money, only represent
Its value, which we know full-well,
　　Is but, as 'tis in commerce meant.

For, 'tis a dead and useless thing,
　　Unless put into workers' hands,
Where its true value, it will bring,
　　And he works best who understands

That all the wealth of all the world,
　　Is vested in the laboring class,
And our star-banner is unfurled,
　　Dipped to their honor, as they pass.

Begrimed with toil, they honored, are,
  A-sweat and weary, bent and worn,
They have of all, the holiest share,
  Of right — nor shall it e'er be torn

From them, nor shall the laborer be,
  In working clothes, e'er set aside,
By nabobs, who the toiling see,
  While in their carriage, they may ride.

But they, the wage-workers, are not
  To think they have the right to say
That 'tis their right, and only lot,
  To dictate, fully all their pay,

They may o'er-charge, they surely may
  Be under-paid, and, 'tis of force,
That caution's needed, every way,
  That what is right they'll have, of course.

And all must " live and let live," too,
  And neither be, at all unjust,
But keep this motto still in view,
  IF ONE GOES DOWN, THE OTHER MUST.

And 'tis by mutual charity,
   And mutual interest, all can live,
And there is no disparity,
   That each must, to the other, give.

Employer and employee, both,
   Are bound to see, the righteous thing
Is, done, and neither be so loth,
   As to refuse his skill to bring,

To make all fair and equal, so
   Neither does over-reach, nor fail
This right and privilege, well to show,
   And, in his right to, well-prevail.

And why not? Should there be the test
   Of money, lands, or, palace grand,
As reason why *that* man is best,
   Who has these ready at command?

No; character and honest toil, —
   Brain, Brawn, are what are most of worth,
And who has these, has power to foil,
   All charges of inferior birth.

COTTAGE AND PALACE.

The humble home — where comfort dwells,
   And peace sits smiling all the day,
Where sweet contentment always tells,
   How pleasant, 'tis there thus to stay,

Where wife prepares the table — where
   The children, kempt and well-behaved,
Where all the family has share
   In the spread board — with blessing craved:

Where God is honored — and the Book
   Is read, and daily prayer is heard;
That is the place where one may look;
   'Tis like the nest of singing bird.

And 'tis a palace, just as grand,
   As marble, brownstone, granite, glass;
As good as any in the land;
   Fit, note of angels, as they pass.

If there, economy is used,
   And habits, bad, are all eschewed,
And manhood, never is abused,
   And every thing, and act, reviewed,

So that the *best*, may *first* be done,
    And what *must be*, with hope, is borne,
Though burdening, till life's race is run,
    And Heaven's Eternal Crown is worn,

Then, 'tis enough, and he is wise,
    Who loves that sweet and holy spot;
Who sees it, till it fills his eyes,
    And, for a better, careth not.

Economy, to him, *is* wealth;
    'Tis better than a mine of gold;
'Tis better than the funds of stealth;
    Its value is not ready told.

And skill to work, is tariff high;
    Protection, is for faithful toil,
And he forbids dread want come nigh,
    Who burns economic, his oil.

If men are frugal, they can live
    On less than spendthrifts can afford,
And then, to charity, can give
    A mite, and keep a well-filled board.

The most men lack is common sense,
  The knowledge of the common laws,
To save some foolish, vain expense,
  And know when they for courts, have cause.

We need an old JOHN ADAMS, now;
  A Socrates, or Plato, who
Can teach the people, daily, how
  They best, and wisest work, may do.

Some Seneca, to teach the truth,
  Some Spartan law to train our boys,
Some more and better things for youth,
  Than what, is muscular and noise.

Far better, sense and knowledge is,
  Than skill in games, and athlete limbs,
Than bruising, each, the other's phiz;
  And, thus, to suit ambition's whims.

Laying these paltry things, aside,—
  The use of tricks, and frauds, and rings,
Not on ambition's nag to ride,
  Which oft, his rider, earthward flings,

We must the thoughts of people mould,
    That, with full-care, — the ship of state,
May well be manned, and her course hold,
    And keep off from the rocks of fate.

That, as the waves dash furiously,
    Which threaten her with instant doom,
She may ride safely through the sea,
    Though clouds may gather, with thick gloom.

The times are full of danger-signs,
    There's not enough of sober thought,
Too much, the younger blood inclines,
    To be, in wayward channels, caught.

Sport, play, the base-ball, and the dance,
    The horse-race, yacht-race, club, and fair,
The ticket, with the lot and chance,
    Are things, alas, not few nor rare.

'Twas thus, when Babylon went down;
    Thus, when Rome fell from her high place;
Thus, with Pompeii's fated town;
    Thus may it be in our own case.

ALL EQUAL BEFORE THE LAW.

We must, our fathers' principles
   Make ours, and keep them, ever pure,
In State, and in Municipals;
   Else we cannot, through time, endure.

The Bible foremost, sure, must be;
   Our country, Christian, first was named,
And sad, will be, the day we see,
   When " 'tis *not* Christian," shall be claimed.

Our schools must be forever free,
   No parochial, or sect-schools, can,
Into our school's place come, and we
   Must stand up to this, to a man.

All men before the law, must, still
   Be equal, as at first, and right
Must still prevail, with strong good-will,
   Nor be out-flanked, by wrong and might.

This is thy teaching, John, I know,
   Thy kindly heart did ever feel
For manhood, in its weal or woe;
   The down-crushed, 'neath the tyrant's heel,

For common weal is commonwealth,
    We cherish Commonwealth, our own,
And for our good and perfect health,
    We must protect it, zone to zone.

    ...   .

Well, here thou art worn in thy years,
    And seeking rest, and quietude;
Not wanting that which interferes,
    And does into thy thought, intrude,

Yet, whilst thou sittest down, serene,
    And layest pen and themes aside,
And shadows, falling, intervene,
    And heaven's doors seem opening wide,

To let thee see the home beyond,
    Where shines the bright eternal day,
Of which thy heart is cheerly fond,
    For which thou dost devoutly pray,

Perchance I may, mean time, relate
    Something of this, less life, of mine,
And, in my measure, simply state,
    What it may have to do with thine.

THE BIRTHDAY BOWER.

The birthdays intervined, entwine
   Together, running, thus, along,
Like twisted clinging, eglantine,
   Making an arbor, green and strong,

And flowering, as the fragrant rose,
   Delighting every well-taught sense,
Which, thus, its pleasure-power shows,
   To hold the while, in pleased suspense.

So, whilst thou sittest here, awhile,
   I will a moment, briefly stay,
And watch thy face, thy kindly smile,
   As of myself a word I say.

My life has been eventful, still
   It has not been my lot to stand
Where, I, the highest place could fill,
   Among the nobles of the land.

No crown of laurels decks my brow;
   I sit, not yet, where praises greet
My ear, I'm only doing, now,
   Whate'er I can, with weary feet.

I fold not yet, across my breast,
  My hands, to bid the world "*good-night*,"
I am not ready, yet to rest;
  I still would battle for the right,

But health is under-weather, some,
  And pains are keeping me in mind, —
As slyly they do go and come,
  And treat me in a way unkind,

That I am mortal, and my feet,
  Shall one day stop their weary walk,
At Way-side Inn, and, I shall meet,
  The crowd, that, long, have ceased to talk;

The silent crowd, laid down to sleep,
  Where the white stones their berths disclose,
Where Angel-porters, guard-watch keep,
  Where none the others' presence, knows.

But now I'm living, and I know,
  As know all living, I must die,
And that, while living, much I owe,
  To God, and man, and, I will try

DOING WHAT I CAN.

To do my part, that I may be
    Of some use, while I here remain,
For, if I fail, I do not see,
    How, ever, I'll come back again

To mend a path's bad crookedness,
    Or place the steps, if turned aside,
Aright, nor, any soul to bless,
    Where I did, foretime, but deride.

I know, but weakly, I can do,
    Whatever work my hands may find,
But I would be, to right most true,
    And, to my fellow-men, most kind.

So, with my might, whate'er my hands
    Find to do, I'll, the best I can,
Do, thus to strengthen friendship's bands,
    And bless my needy fellow-man.

" For there's no knowledge in the grave,
    Work or device," where all-we, go,
Not there, can one, his neighbor save,
    " For all the dead, do, nothing know."

I'm but a Gospel minister, sir,
    For many years I've tried to preach,
And I have sought, as I aver,
    In Christ's dear name men's hearts to reach,

To bid the lost, whom Christ has found,
    To look to Him, the Crucified,
Who, with the thorns was rudely crowned,
    As, on Mount Calvary, He died.

To bid the prodigal return,
    Rag-clothed, to find a welcome home,
That, that fond heart, which now doth yearn,
    Shall know he doth no longer roam.

To tell the wandering boys, who stray,
    From the old roof-tree of their birth,
How mother, still, at home, doth pray,
    And wait, at that dear spot of earth.

To see them come, with hands still clean,
    And souls as pure as childhood's, so,
They, free from deeds depraved and mean,
    Still may, that mother's welcome, know.

To help believers keep the faith;
    To show how reason doth bestow,
Light, on whate'er the Almighty saith,
    And thus how faith may reason, know.

To tell the world of future things,
    Which inspiration hath revealed,
Of what the Christ, at coming, brings,
    Which has for ages been concealed.

How prophecy, has shed its light,
    A-down the ages, till we see,
A radiance shining, clear and bright,
    Upon the page of history.

That, as the tenon deftly fits
    The mortise, so, the Prophecy,
Just the Historic statement hits,
    That one may well the fitness see.

And say, "this is that spoken" by the Lord,
    Who by his servant Faithful, spoke,
And thus has kept his truthful word,
    That never, once, its truth-line broke.

So I have said, " behold the time,
   Is fast approaching, and the day,
When, coming in his might, sublime,
   The Christ shall hold, on earth, his sway."

But, while I've wrought, my life has sped,
   For fifty-five, full-rounded years,
And friends are numbered with the dead,
   And I have swung 'twixt smiles and tears,

Like pendulum; most poisely hung;
   First one, then other; then the one;
And thus, has sped, as songs are sung,
   This life, and soon it may be done.

How swiftly speed these years; 'tis short
   The time, since I was but a boy,
And all seems but a thing of naught,
   Since first I played in careless joy.

So, like "a weaver's shuttle" swift;
   Or, like "a tale that's briefly told,"
Or, like the autumn leaves that drift,
   When winds are blowing, bleak and cold.

YOUTH–POVERTY NO DAMAGE.

I think-me now, of youthful days,
   Which I spent in my poverty,
And since have held my own; my lays,
   Are sung midst what I *hope* to see.

But I am most content; I **know**,
   No Potentate of earth is throned
So high as he, who, thus, can show,
   He is, of God, in such case, owned.

And I am rich in this estate,
   Though poor enough in coffered wealth;
My Father-God is rich and great,
   And what care I for worldly pelf?

The heir of millions cannot show,
   Though he has wealth in boundless store,
Such riches, in their overflow;
   Such having, one can ask no more.

So, spending youth in poverty,
   Is not a damage to a boy,
For better poor than rich, is he,
   For then, he must, his *powers* employ.

On, up to school, with ready feet,
    I went, old *Craneneck* marked the way,
And took my knife-hacked, paintless seat,
    Intent on study, more than play.

Outside, I had the hardest time,
    The boys made me their special jest,
And, in positions not sublime,
    I oft was placed, *beneath the rest.*

"A pile, a pile!" was oft the shout,
    The signal for the rush, pell-mell,
When every boy, where'er about,
    Helped, up, a "pile," grotesque, to swell.

"A *pile*" it *was*, of arms and legs,
    Looking like some grim monster, huge,
Made of waste pieces, prongs and pegs,
    Before the days of the deluge.

They screamed and shouted, while I lay,
    Down, under all, in sorry plight,
Breathless and panting; I did pray
    That I might be relieved out-right.

I cried, "Oh! boys, do let me out!
　　I'm almost dead, I cannot breathe!"
But they cared not, they were about
　　Their play, nor would me, then relieve.

I was but small — I could not do
　　The fighting, to keep up my end,
So, it, my physique oft did rue,
　　Almost without a helping friend.

But, in the school-room, I could keep
　　My place a-top, and hold my own;
They could not "*pile*" on me their heap;
　　My bench was to me as a throne.

And yet, oft-times, on me was laid
　　The blame of what the others did,
And I, their scape-goat, thus, was made,
　　And, for them, I was often, chid.

So they colluded and conspired,
　　To get each other rid of blame,
And get for me what they desired;
　　Not feeling for it proper shame.

A story I will here relate,
    How, once, such deed was almost done,
But not quite — I was saved the fate,
    Which sometimes came of their sweet fun.

One day a boy I will not name,
    For, living yet, he may not care
To have it told. — 'Tis just the same,
    As I, the truth, most sure, declare;

One day he, Yankee, with his knife
    The benches whittled, — (nothing new;
There seemed among the boys a strife
    To see which, most, such work would do;

For those pine benches, without paint,
    Were made the test of all the knives,
And many a cut and carving, quaint,
    Was made, though nothing now survives;

For that old house has gone, and all
    The deeds done to it, have gone, too,
And only can our thought recall
    Its form; we had another, new.)

This boy used his own knife until
    The teacher took it; then he sought
Another, trying whittling still,
    And was, in this deed, likewise, caught.

He borrowed knives, until the desk
    (High in the corner) showed a pile,
He, running quite a little risk,
    Of something-else — after a while.

That teacher had an easy way;
    He would not *whip* — *until he must;*
And, thus he failed, most every day,
    To deal a penalty, most just.

So this bad boy, still whittled on,
    And borrowed knives from all around,
Until, most all the knives had gone,
    Where others, their duress, had found.

I sat behind him. Turning back
    He whispered, "Ask George for *his* knife";
That moment I, some sense did lack,
    (It has been so, sometimes, in life.)

So I asked George, behind me, "Lend
    Your knife to him;" at once George spoke,
Telling the teacher. He no friend
    Was, to the boys who, school-rules, broke.

I was exposed, and, then, I said,
    As honest as I well could be,
And, as best, then, my school-boy head
    The true way out, could safely see;

I said, "*He asked me to.*" "A lie,
    I didn't," cried he, who, before,
Had asked the knife, — so, did deny;
    And what could I say then? No more.

So I was sandwiched in between
    That boy and he who sat behind;
I thought, it might be plainly seen,
    That *he* had "lied," by one not blind.

The teacher knew what had been done,
    How, knives, he'd taken, half a score,
And, that, perchance, another one
    Might, yet, be added to *his* store.

Logic is logic, and as plain
    As, "two and two are four," the truth
Was evident, that, once, again,
    A knife was wanted by that youth.

In any court, good evidence
    Would be, *the knives the teacher had;*
And *any* teacher, with right sense,
    Could make a case against that lad.

But, sometimes policy gets place;
    Justice is pushed at once, aside;
We see that Policy will trace,
    And know the evil, far and wide.

That teacher was a good man, though;
    He prayed in school, day after day;
He would not do a wrong, to know
    That he had failed, in any way,

But he was like some *other* men,
    Who are afraid to speak right out,
And keep themselves, reticent, when,
    Their interests, they must, nowise, flout.

He was like Pilate ; Herod ; men,
    Who, though the right they well could see,
Were ready to be weak-kneed, when
    Somebody would more pleasèd be.

Such, like, so well, " to please the Jews,"
    And keep themselves good friends with those
Whose friendship they may wish to use,
    Whose will they do not dare oppose.

So, justice fails, through cowards ; men,
    Who should be firm, are limp and weak,
And when they should be firmest, then
    They with a faltering softness, speak.

That teacher, somewhat like this was ;
    He spoke out, in a kind, mild way,
Most non-committal, with a pause,
    And did, with show of fairness, say : —

" Well, boys, 'tis difficult to tell
    Just where the truth, in this case, lies —
Somewhere between you is its spell,
    And, who knows where it is, is wise.

"*I* cannot tell, perhaps one wise
  As Solomon, could find it. I
Cannot, with all my powers, devise
  A way to do it, and won't try."

He named me ; said the truth I'd told,
  Once, when against myself it bore ;
Then left the case ; — I was consoled,
  Although, he might have helped me more.

(" Not proven " — is a verdict, made
  By Scotland's jury, when they find
That evidence is not arrayed,
  So, " GUILTY," they, the accused, can bind.

It lets him go, and, yet, the dark
  Suspicion rests upon the man ;
And, everywhere, men, willing, hark
  To hear against him, what they can.)

So I was with suspicion held,
  Though I had "*sometimes*" told the truth,
And I was, by the means, compelled,
  The lie, to share with *that* frail youth,

But 'tis far better to be thought
  A liar, when the truth is told,
Than, in a lie to be close-caught,
  And manhood, thus be, cheaply, sold.

For, conscious of integrity,
  One can, suspicioned, lift his head;
But, he who KNOWS he lies, must be
  A cringing coward-knave, instead:

Unless, as, mostly, liars are
  Lost to all shame, and, careless, quite;
Their brazen faces show no care,
  For they are *rather* wrong than right.

I'd told the truth, that, well, I knew,
  And, that the *other boy*, did lie,
But, still it lay *between us two*,
  And it might be *that boy*, or . . *I*.

So, time went on, and I ofttimes,
  Did feel the blow upon my back,
For others, who, to hide their crimes,
  Caused me to get the birch-rod whack.

MOTHER'S SYMPATHY.

When, *of themselves,* they should have told,
   And, so, have told the better truth;
But, rarely were the boys so bold;
   They rather tell of me, forsooth.

But, still I studied, and I learned
   My lessons, by some hook or crook,
For oh! my soul with high hope, yearned,
   To know the contents of my book.

But I, at home, had sympathy;
   My mother was my dearest friend,
And, always she encouraged me,
   And did, her hopeful spirit lend,

To help me on my hapless way,
   Though, oft, I almost wished me dead;
But she, some cheering word would say,
   While pillowing on her breast, my head,

"Go, study, do not mind the boys;
   Who studies will not be a fool;
Play makes them dull and mere toys;
   Go, my dear boy, still go to school."

So cheered she me, day after day,
   And I kept on, and spelled and read,
And all my lessons learned to say,
   Whether in class, at foot or head.

But head of class is where the best
   And brightest of the scholars, stands,
No matter where may stand the rest;
   The best, the headship well commands.

And 'twas not always at the head,
   The teachers left, the best could be;
The column, sometimes, there was led,
   By some one's sons, not me, d'ye see.

But though the favored ones did stand
   Above me, by some scheme, there-placed,
Yet, oft, I could the place demand
   And constantly I, it, menaced.

Sometimes I got it, for a while,
   And, sometimes, lost it, by mishap;
Either of right, or trap of guile,
   I yielded to some other chap.

A CONFLICT.

Once, I was nearly at the foot,
   One, only stood below me, when
A word (it might have been, SURTOUT,)
   Was missed, I spelled it right, and, then, —

The teacher gave it to the next,
   Who spelled it right, just as I had,
Then up he went, — I was sore vexed,
   And went and stood above that lad.

I was quite hasty, — I was not
   A perfect boy, — and I was sure,
The place was mine; alas! I got
   Something, my imprudence to cure,

A conflict with the teacher? Yes,
   I should have, rather, kept my place,
(As if, the word, I then did miss,)
   And suffer it — if in disgrace.

I had my knuckles rapped by him
   Who laid me in the lie before,
The teacher bade him — rather slim
   Was the pretext — a bad work's score.

No boy in school should e'er rebel,
  Although he may not get his rights;
It never does of honor tell,
  When one his teacher, daring, fights,

But I felt well my right, and knew
  I suffered wrongfully, and claimed
The head, and, so, I sought to do,
  What, as an act, was to be blamed.

Once, when a little fellow, I
  Sat in my seat, a class was out
Spelling, and every one did try
  To spell *Squash*, but each, lagging lout

Failed, I put my hand up, and caught
  The teacher's eye, I spelled the word;
Just as those bigger scholars ought;
  And somewhat, then, their ire stirred.

I was a child — it pleased me then,
  That I could spell a class-missed word,
How much I was like most of men,
  Of such, as you, sir, oft have heard,

THE LOVE OF VICTORY.

Who, pleaséd are, with victory,
   And love to know they've beaten those
Who failed of what they sought to be, —
   Then, blatantly, their joy expose.

Not much like that fair girl, who said,
   " I'm sorry that the word I spelled,"
And thus her boy-friend comforted;
   And thus, his rising feeling quelled.

"I love you," was the reason why,
   And love will conquer vanity;
For it, a friend will, for you, die;
   He, conqueror, cannot, conquered be.

But, yet, there is in every heart
   The love of victory, and the soul
Will from life, even, gladly part,
   That it may reach the victor's goal.

It is not wrong, if never gained,
   Through cause of other's purposed fall;
If none are by it, wilfully pained,
   Then one may go before them all.

I never sought a place to gain,
    By crowding other men aside;
I would not cause another pain;
    I'd sooner *walk* that one might *ride*,

Than throw him off, and vault his steed,
    And leave him, bruised and in the dust;
Such course is but the spur of greed,
    And whoso does, is slave to lust.

The road is open for the boy,
    And open for the girl, — for all,
And whoso will, may know the joy,
    Which comes at honest Victor's call.

I sought that road, as best I could,
    Sometimes had friends, sometimes, alone;
Not always right, or, always good,
    For faults I had, I'm free to own.

Sometimes my teachers helped me on;
    My teacher, MARY, was that sort;
On me she did not look with scorn,
    Although she whipped me, when she ought.

MY FRIEND HENRY.

In ripe good age, she liveth still,
   Genial and pleasant, grace-wise bred;
And, late, she with a kind, good will,
   To me, "You had your lessons," said.

I had a friend, too, in the school,
   Henry, a boy above my age,
Who kept the teacher's strictest rule,
   And, as my champion did engage.

He lives to-day, on the old place,
   Where he lived then, the only one,
In all that district — who I trace
   To that old schoolhouse, — all are gone.

And still our friendship holds its sway,
   Through all these years of toil and pain,
And, if we part at last, some day,
   The hope will be, to meet again.

True friendships last, thus, through the years;
   Through sun and storm, in devious way;
They share the smiles and share the tears,
   Each of the other, day by day.

Begun in boyhood, how these keep,
    The heart still fresh, while all around,
Is bleak and cold, and many sleep,
    Who once we loved, 'neath grassy mound.

Yes, friendship once, when rooted fast,
    Is not a plant that soon must die,
It stands and grows, through stormy blast,
    And does all jealousy, defy.

'Tis death, alone, can separate
    The friends, who, here, are strongly bound,
And there's a place where, mate to mate,
    True friends will meet, on holiest ground.

" Blest be the tie," the poet sung,
    "That binds our hearts in purest love;"
" Blest be the tie," sings every tongue,
    That binds friends — as they're bound above.

    . . .   .

In school, I learned things far ahead
    Of classes; I could " conjugate,"
" Decline," and, oft, I, better, read,
    Than those who did my poor self, hate.

I spoke my pieces too, and felt
  Thrilled by the words, whose deep-toned sense
Made my heart, sympathetic, melt,
  Or thrill with joyfulness intense.

I spoke Bozzaris, storied brave;
  I spoke The Brussels Ball; The Death
Of Ashmun; The African Slave;
  The African Chief, with heated breath.

The Negro's sad Complaint, I spake,
  How he was forced from home, to toil,
Which, every tie of love did break;
  It made my blood, with ire, boil.

I, thus, first gained my hatred, deep,
  For slavery, and its cruelties,
Which, well could make the angels weep,
  And, of the pit of Satan, is.

Cowper and Whittier, to me
  Were men whose souls, into my own
Poured their deep feeling, I could see
  Each slave's sad lot, hear every groan.

I heard men argue for the rights
    Of wrong, — no rights it ever had ;
And who such wrong's rights proudly cites,
    Must sure be daft, or, else, be mad.

What are the rights of slavery ? I
    Asked, and my soul said, none ;
Not one thing right, could I descry,
    When I, the best, my work had done.

So felt I, and that sense I prize,
    Because it, early, sat me right ;
It opened so my boyish eyes,
    So, ever, as its foe, I'd fight.

Thus was it, when, were hunted down,
    Both Burns and Sims, in Boston, where,
In that grand, old Historic town,
    Men, 'gainst oppression did declare,

And their great harbor, curtly made,
    A tea-pot for King George ye Third,
For a salt-tea ; Red Men arrayed,
    Did, what-of, men, world-wide have heard.

And Bunker Hill, and Lexington,
    And Concord, all are witness, how,
The victory, by the fight was won,
    When freemen proud, refused to bow.

King George, might drink his cup of tea,
    And make wry faces, if he pleased,
It meant oppressors, such as he,
    Should, thus, in all his goods be seized,

And overboard be quickly thrown,
    Because the sense of innate right
Could not, the right of power condone,
    The rights of freemen thus to smite.

And, thus, oppression was, to me,
    Whate'er its form, a hateful thing,
I, ever, 'gainst its cause must be,
    I would, aside, its false claims fling.

The FUGITIVE SLAVE LAW, accursed,
    Was a most monstrous thing, and vile;
Of all our laws it was the worst,
    Enacted of men's, wile and guile.

Men claimed that the great, Federal power,
    Should not o'er Southern States, be held;
But, what of Northern States, that hour,
    Which, us to return their slaves, compelled?

When those black men, for refuge came,
    Burns, Sims, up hither, to the north,
And were returned, I felt the shame,
    And, I confess it, I was wroth.

With those poor men my sympathy
    Was placed, as thine, good friend, and thou
Didst say right words, that men might see,
    How vile the curse that made them bow,

Not them, alone, for all were held
    Subservient to that evil power,
That law which did, its fetters weld
    On all the north, that fearful hour.

No wonder we were filled with shame,
    That such a law was ever passed,
And loathed its very phase, and name;
    Thank God it did no long-while, last,

THE PRAYER-CRY.

But those poor blacks, were sorely held
    In the strong fetters, of the sin,
Which bound the burden, and compelled,
    Them, still, to work the cotton-gin,

And rice swamps, and the cotton fields
    Where bloomed the bolls like lilies fair
The fragrance they could only yield,
    Was the poor, burdened toiler's prayer

And I, though far-off, heard the cry,
    As he, in anguish, plead with God;
As though the supplicant would die,
    Beneath the scourging of the rod.

One could not utter deeper tone,
    More full of bitter agony,
Though dying, on far-isle, alone,
    Where only God, his woe could see.

I hear that cry to-day, as though
    It came afresh, from that sad soul;
For, still it echoes, and I know
    It will, through endless ages, roll:

Roll, as a heaven-sent word of truth,
    Whence, still, the guilt and blame remains,
Which held, within the awful ruth,
    The slave, in his hard, galling chains.

The prayer was; " Let us, captib's, go;
    We perish here, beneath dis load,
Dou dost, our fearful sufferin's, know,
    Wid dis, our hard task-master's goad.

Oh, break dese fetters, dat so long
    Hab boun' us, tearin' our poor flesh,
Oh! Lord, dou knows we suffer wrong,
    An', how our tears, each day, flow fresh.

Oh, brung de year ob jubilo,
    An' set us slabes, foreber free;
Oh, let us, from dis bondage go;
    Oh, hear us, as we cry to de.

Dou didst, dy chillen, brung, dry shod,
    By Moses' han', tro de Red Sea,
When, ober it, he hel' his rod;
    Oh set us, Lord, in dat way, free.

THE SLAVE'S PRAYER.

Gib us a Moses, let his han',
    Lead us, dry-shod tro de sea-red;
Oh, gib dy great supreme comman',
    And let us be, by Moses led.

Our wibes (dey *ours* de bes', *we know*)
    Our chillen, — all from us are torn,
An' here we dem shal' know no mo',
    Dey are, to some lan', from us borne.

Dey's sol' from us, for Massa's gold,
    Made outen our own brains and blood,
Warm, whil' our Massa's hearts are *cold*,
    Like Phar'o's, harden' against God.

Lord, we mus' hab our liberty,
    We mus' be, from dis Egyp' led,
For here dine eyes can surely see,
    Dat we, here, *just as good as dead.*

Now let dy serbants go, we pray,
    Keep off de blood-houn's from our track,
And let us not go far astray;
    Turn us not from de right way, back.

De Norf star tells us where de lan',
　'Flowing wid milk and honey' be;
Oh take us, by dy friendly han',
　And brung us to sweet liberty."

Thus, as in vision, I heard pray,
　The slave, it made my sore heart ache,
I prayed that God would take away,
　His chains, and, free, for Jesu's sake.

So, as those words, deep-pierced my soul,
　I longed to see the oppressor's rod
Broken, that, off from him might roll,
　His burdens, by the hand of God.

Thank God, the deed is done, at last,
　The end of slavery has come,
And its dark days are, long since, passed,
　And every braying dog is dumb.

Those fetters are all broken now,
　That auction-block is now no more;
Beneath that lash slaves do not bow,
　Nor feel their backs lash-cut and sore.

THE BROKEN FETTERS.

The deed is done, — that *Red Sea* passed,
   Red with the blood of slain men, who
Fought for the Union till the last,
   Till Moses led the hosts all through.

'Twas a long strife, that civil (?) war;
   It made thee, man of peace, turn pale,
So much did thy kind heart abhor
   Its horrors, but thou didst not quail.

But I, a while was in the strife,
   Was mingling in those scenes of blood,
Where Rebel minions sought our life,
   And stained, with blood, the soil we trod,

They fired on our flag, as well
   Theirs, (though they did, another, fly;)
The old flag which so well did tell,
   How once our fathers, fought, to die.

We turn back to the gloomy days,
   When, clouds of darkness o'er us hung,
And note how, by the stormy ways,
   At length, our victory, we sung.

We "waited 'neath the furnace blast;"
    The fearful heat, until, anew,
We, like the Hebrew's, it's flame past,
    And came out, to our country true.

That Traitor-Leader, Davis, he,
    Was Satan's minion, to up-hold
The "sacred institution,"(?) we
    In him, a Judas, once more, see.

He worshiped at the black-god's shrine,
    A craven, devotee; his cause,
To him was all things, most divine;
    For that, he did defy our laws.

He, recreant to his Country's flag,
    Led on his proud, rebellious host,
Who, 'neath that flouting, rebel rag,
    Made most presumptuous, reckless boast.

This boast, their roll full-soon they'd call,
    On Bunker Hill, the roll of slaves,
Where that strong granite's, shadows fall,
    Upon the green-grown patriots' graves,

But, vain the boast, for, they did yield;
    Their cause was not the cause of right,
Though, valiantly, they took the field,
    And did, against their country fight.

They claimed *state rights*, as the excuse,
    For their rebellion, but they meant,
The right to hold their slaves, and use
    Them, without Federal consent.

Though that consent they had, at first,
    By compromise, Missouri, called,
But, soon that bad-claim-bubble burst,
    And all their hearts were much appalled.

The chains of that great power we broke;
    The burdened captives were set free,
For Lincoln held the pen, whose stroke
    Proclaimed, the year of jubilee.

Lincoln, that name how white and fair
    It shines, undimming, through the years;
A name, like Washington's, most rare,
    To be proclaimed through all the spheres.

An honest man, full-souled, was he,
    Of kindly heart, and nerve of steel;
He took that pen, and dared to be,
    Slavery's destroyer, Freedom's weal.

That Proclamation did the deed,
    Emancipation had its right,
And, thus, our bondmen, all, were freed;
    Banished, was slavery's gloomy night.

Would he had lived to know how well
    He struck that fatal, deadly blow;
But we, who live, forever shall,
    His work, in all its grandness, know.

Oh! shameful deed, so full of hate,
    Of Wilkes Booth, which we here record,
Only to speak of Lincoln's fate;
    And speak of his high-prized reward.

We note Booth's deed, but to condemn;
    Nor he, nor any other man,
Can, thus, dare raise a hand, for then,
    They bring God's curse, upon their plan.

Sic Semper Tyrannis, cannot
    Prove one a tyrant; nor condone,
The act, which is a deed whose blot,
    Shall rest upon that soul, alone.

Oh! Lincoln, Lincoln; even now
    Our grief for him, is hard to bear,
While, still, in tearful mood, we bow,
    And weeds of mourning, heart-grieved, wear.

Blest be his memory, and curst
    Be he who smote him down;
Wilkes Booth is named among the worst,
    While Lincoln wears a fadeless crown;

Crown of a Nation's honor, bright,
    And brighter growing, day by day;
While Booth's name dims to darkest night,
    With stigma, on it, hence, for aye.

Well is it, we have had good men,
    Who, needed were, at such a time,
To work for right, with voice and pen,
    According with God's work, sublime.

They die, but live on in their deeds,
    And what they do, with brightest sheen,
Shines on, and their life-record reads,
    Immortal, their death-lines between.

We see it, as the time rolls on,
    When each new phase of things appears,
When, as the old days, hence, are gone,
    The new come on, with march of years.

A Man is needed; lo! 'tis he
    Who then appears, to, destined, stand,
Where he of service, grand may be,
    Like one born, duly, close at hand.

'Twas so with Lincoln, he stood where
    The angry powers, together, clashed,
And, midst the lightning's lurid glare,
    As steel and flint, together flashed.

There was he, just the man to do,
    What, scarce another, would have done,
When, thus to be, to right, so true,
    Was not the guise of every one.

And well it was a Party knew,
    Just at that time, what man to choose,
And, just what freemen ought to do,
    And how, the ballot best to use.

The nation now, with high acclaim,
    May speak of Lincoln, and rejoice,
But, first, Republicans, did name,
    And make him, their best, chiefest choice.

That grand old Party, ever true
    To its behests, still standeth strong,
Ready, its noble work to do;
    Oh! may it stand, right-faced, and long,

With honor, principle, and just,
    To hold the helm of our grand Ship;
For, guided by one-else, she must
    Against the rocks, most hapless, slip.

True to the cause of home and land;
    True to the temperance cause, to be;
The grand, old Host, — with high command,
    Must lead us still to victory.

For we have interests, still, of worth,
　　Questions of vast import arise,
And everywhere, from all the earth,
　　Are turned to us a billion eyes.

Jeff Davis; now has gone, at last,
　　Death, with *his* mandate, doth prevail,
And he who held slaves' bonds so fast,
　　Is held by bonds that will not fail

To hold *him*, unreleasing, while
　　The years go on, majestic by,
Until, is heard through age's aisle,
　　The blast of judgment-trumpet, high.

But, while he's dead, and slavery, too,
　　And nevermore the curse, we'll feel,
There comes to us a question, new,
　　Which shows how slowly wounds do heal;

The question, whether, now, the men
　　Who first, as slaves to us were brought,
And wrought a hundred years, and, then,
　　By every, slave-bond, were well-taught,

How to obey, with unpaid toil,
   And *earn* their *Master's* daily bread;
Tilling the ever friendly soil;
   Not owning cover for the head, —

Whether, they, *now* shall here remain,
   Or, go to Africa, since, now,
Is broken, their hard, galling chain;
   Since, hence, to master they'll ne'er bow,

" We have no further use for them,
   They've out-lived usefulness, and they
Must know their black skin, does condemn,
   And they must up, and go away."

But they *are here*, and have their rights,
   The highest rights of all, to be
Before the law, equal, — and might's
   High presage is their royalty.

They must protected be, to stay
   Or go, at will, as other men;
To choose their place, as best they may,
   Nor be coerced, or bound again.

We want no law to bid them *go*,
  Nor make their stay unpleasant here;
They must, with all our people, know,
  That they can stay, with happy cheer,

To earn their bread, to be *men*, all,
  As others, who their equals are,
Equal to all, whom we can call
  Our countrymen here, 'neath stripe and star;

To educate their children here,
  To *vote* as they may, self-forced, choose,
And never feel a cringing fear,
  When they, their franchise-right, shall use.

Thus far has triumphed their boon-right;
  Thus far they, in their manhood, stand;
And right protected is, by might
  Of all the armies of our land.

And still the march is on, and still,
  The progress is toward the day,
When, everywhere, that people will
  Have right, to, unmolested, stay.

THE RACE-WAR FOOLISH. 109

Why not? Why seek to drive them off?
    Why think our white-skin or blue-blood,
Is reason at them thus, to scoff,
    As though we were superior mud?

Go to; let's stop this arrant claim;
    Go, look on death, see how, alike,
No matter what the race or name,
    Death does, with equal blow, all strike.

'Tis foolish, this race-war, this feud;
    This most unrighteous, unjust claim;
And only those who are imbued
    With evil, such a course will name.

Now so far we have come, to know
    The old-time fetter-clank, has gone,
And much to thee, good man, we owe,
    As still our cause is marching on.

And thou hast lived to see the time,
    When, thus, athwart the eastern sky,
There shines the omen-star sublime,
    Which heralds that glad day, most nigh,

And cheerful words I bring to thee,
   In these, thy days of feeble age,
The thanks of millions, who must be,
   Thy Galaxy of friends — good sage.

Let us be hopeful God still lives;
   Justice and judgment His high throne
Inhabit, and He always gives
   His aid, to those who, His cause, own.

Thou hast the Freedman's cause espoused,
   And not alone *his* cause, for thou
Hast, ever, thy just soul aroused,
   For all who burdened, low did bow.

See who, in thorny pathways, knew
   The hardships of a bitter lot,
Who, to their conscience-faith were true,
   Who suffered, yet upbraided not.

The hunted outcasts, who, thus bore,
   The stigma, with no quiet rest,
Driven, like dumb dogs from the door;
   By woes and ills sorely oppressed.

Their only crime — their "*thee*" and "*thou*";
    Their harmless, non-resisting way;
Their faith that, they must worship how,
    Their conscience taught, God-moved, to pray.

The hot-head bigot-zealots, wild,
    Who thought, God-service they did do,
As they the innocents reviled,
    Were by thy pen brought full to view,

Their portraits thou didst draw, to life,
    With every lineament clearly traced,
To show of what their souls were rife,
    With all the good heart-lines derased.

Good men, *perhaps* they were, like Saul,
    Who, armed with warrants, chased the saints
Unto Damascus, but, the Paul,
    Aside set Saul, by God's restraints.

It takes sometimes a lightning flash,
    Which first may blind the zealot's eyes,
Then, after that loud thunder-crash,
    The scales may fall to his surprise.

So he may see, as ne'er before,
    What-of, his conscience-work was made,
And, like that Saul, he may deplore,
    That he made good men thus afraid.

God uses men like thee, to do
    Such work, as will, at length, avail,
And thou hast been, to thy work, true,
    Although men did like dæmons rail.

Thou didst well-champion the cause,
    Of those who were, of rights denied,
E'en, when against them, stood the laws,
    By which they were severely tried.

Laws framed, to do them, unjust hurt,
    And, though they lived lives, spotless, pure,
They were besmeared, dragged in the dirt,
    Such harmful treatment to endure.

Or, more, chased, banished from their home,
    " By order of the Supreme Court,"
And made, in far-lands, poor, to roam,
    Of beasts and Indians the sport.

Or, hanged for witches in the town
    Of Salem, Puritan and straight
With Orthodoxy's, good renown,
    Yet full of most *un*righteous hate.

So, all, who were suspects, and held,
    To answer to the wondrous test,
By which they were at last, compelled
    To hang, with most religious zest.

Both men and women thus were hanged,
    Wizards and witches; women, who,
If but their tongue a moment clanged,
    Must know how Satan's work to do.

And those poor children, Goodwin's, all
    Who, innocent of crime, were tried,
And felt the blow upon them fall,
    And in their childish prattling, died,

And Roger Sherman, Baptist he,
    Like Quakers, for the faith he held,
Banished, to Providence did flee;
    Being, by unjust laws, compelled.

For cause of such, thy ready word
  Was like, a bugle, clear and strong,
Which, all the world around, is heard;
  A clarion note, condemning wrong.

'Twas all inwrought in thy good verse,
  That, thenceforth, world-wide, mankind, all,
As they the every act rehearse,
  Shall, thee, the Friend of Sufferers, call.

For conscience-freedom thou didst speak,
  That all, to worship, should be free;
Whoever, bowing, soul-full, meek,
  Should, in their rights protected, be.

So, banished Quaker's cause was sung,
  And Goodman Macy's, — at whose door
Come, gray-beard-man, of solemn tongue,
  'Gainst whom the sheriff madly swore.

The blatant sheriff-ruffian, and
  The priest bag-wigged with flowing gown;
Who raced themselves down to the strand,
  Which bordered on old Salisbury's town;

Who thought themselves commissioned, high,
　To do God-service, and to bring
The fleeing back, for courts to try,
　And honor thus, Great George, the King.

Such things were, by thy pen, portrayed,
　And each was held to mirror, true,
Enough to make dæmons afraid,
　And make bad men, their vile deeds rue.

Thou didst protest and cry aloud,
　Against the wrongs, which so distressed;
Against the clamoring, angry crowd;
　Against those who such souls oppressed.

And every sufferer had a friend,
　In thee, and every tyrant knew
That thou, thine aid wouldst, ever, lend,
　Against him, and his wicked crew.

And not for men alone, thy pen,
　Hath been the shining shaft of light;
For, vale and mountain, rock and glen,
　Have found a tongue, as songful Wight.

To sing refrain, though but the voice
   Is known, the echo of thine own;
As though all nature doth rejoice,
   That it shall dwell no more alone.

They have a smoothly cadenced tongue,
   And, beauteous, are with quiet grace,
Since thou hast of them sweetly sung,
   Their legends, in thy lines to trace.

Nothing's too drear or desolate,
   For thee to touch and make it glow,
Thus saving them the direful fate,
   That none, their place, should, ever, know;

Sand-hills and marshes, ponds and bogs,
   The wastes of nature, which the eye
Would turn from, where the tuneful frogs
   Alone would sing — where winds would sigh, —

Have caught the music of thy song,
   Now, with a life-pulse-sense, to thrill,
Echoing through all their scenes, along,
   With thy grand song, their notes to fill.

Some Indian legend, or, perchance,
  Some weird phantasm, Ghoul or Sprite;
Or, fairy's, with fantastic dance;
  Or, Apparition of the night.

" Plumb Island, lies, a whale aground,"
  Stranded along the ocean's shore,
With many a barren sandy mound,
  All verdureless, from days of yore,

And Black Rocks, on the other side,
  And Isles of Shoals, far out at sea,
Where Hamadryads, did abide;
  All owe their fame, poet, to thee.

And up the river, where the tide
  Flows back to Salisbury's, low-marshed shore,
Where Macy's skiff did lightly ride,
  Who took that voyage, unknown before,

And Chain Bridge and Deer Island hold
  A spell thou gavest them in song;
And shores, where dashing billows bold,
  Break all the sandy beach, along.

And Craneneck Hill; and Indian where
  Old Tom, the Great, once held his sway,
Crane Pond and Dole's — with, wonders rare,
  Where pickerel 'neath the pads, oft play.

And Pickerel Pond, in Haverhill Town,
  Hath now. a smoother, softer name,
Kenoza, and a good renown
  It has, though *Pickerel* 'tis, the same.

Never had Craneneck Hill been known,
  Beyond the local home-folk lore;
Nor pond, nor rock, nor tree, could own
  Such classic fame as this, before,

With song thou hast endowed them all,
  Which gives them names, and makes them known,
Till men, the places, curious call,
  And their weird fascinations own.

Thus, all are voiced, by thy sweet art,
  And sing, responsive to thy praise,
And waken, in each senseful heart,
  Voiceful, melodious, joyous lays.

Fame-wide, are now these song-scenes, all
   Associated with thy name,
And light, and shadow, interfall
   A shade a moment, then a flame.

They tell of thee, though first of God,
   Their Great Creator mighty, who
Did, by His fiat and His nod,
   Make all things, at creation, new.

If they can speak of thee, then, I,
   Indebted am, far more than they;
And with them, I would, voiceful, vie,
   In this my humble, kindly, lay,

For thy birthday has given me,
   Allegiance, by the strongest band,
Binding me, this day, to thee,
   With many a silken, woven strand.

I must thus feel the influence, strong,
   Which draws me close to thee, to make
These chords, the chords of sweetest song,
   Whose heart-strings, touched, attuned, awake.

I give to thee my greeting hand,
  I speak my words with friendly voice,
As though I, by thy side, did stand,
  And with thee did, the while, rejoice.

To me thine ever beauteous light,
  Is precious, hence, forever more;
The written years, in letters bright,
  Are Eighteen-Seven, and Thirty-four,

I'll cherish them, as time goes by,
  And drop for thee the kindly tear,
If, first, thou, liest down to die,
  Standing, perchance, beside thy bier,

I'll say, "Blest be the memory
  Of him, the poet of my choice;
Blest be the world, thenceforth, that, he
  Hath uttered, thus, with sweet-toned voice,

His words, poetic, which shall roll,
  Like music through the shining spheres,
To fill each listening, raptured soul,
  With holy joy, while come the years:

MY TRIBUTE.

All full of beauty, by thy lays,
   And resonant with voice of psalm;
As priests, who intertone their praise,
   And wave the green, wide-spreading palm,

Of this, I sing with joy to-day,
   For, who, thus, near thee, but must sing,
Although my feebler, humbler lay,
   Soars not like thine, on lark's high wing.

'Tis but my tribute to thy worth,
   To thy sweet influence, o'er my heart,
Because thy birthday gave me birth:
   For this, I cannot from thee part.

I feel thee near me, sir, to-day,
   This *seventeenth*, the day so rare,
And I will, ever, for thee pray,
   And seek for thee, " OUR FATHER'S " care.

Wilt thou then these lines welcome give,
   These homely lines of kind intent,
That tell how, by this day, I live;
   Since all but for the best are meant?

This day thy precious life began,
    And ran along until I came,
Caught on, and, with it, thenceforth, ran,
    Until it is, to both the same,

And both together, thence are tied,
    In one completed, Gordian knot;
And each, with each, thus close allied,
    Shall never be, through life, forgot,

Thy years now number *eighty-two*,[1]
    My years are *fifty-five*, and we
Have seen our years pass in review,
    Never so many more we'll see.

As runs the glass its swift, still sands,
    So our lives, swiftly speed away,
And near us, possibly, he stands,
    Death's messenger to call, straightway.

And we may never, well-pleased, meet,
    To feel the pressure of each hand,
And, each, the other, kindly greet,
    And, in each other's presence stand.

[1] On Dec. 17, 1889.

I've near thee been, yet it was far,
    I've known thee, — all the while unseen,
Thou Sun, hast been to me a star,
    Since distance did so intervene.

But it was light to me, I feel,
    That, 'tis my light's best radiance, bright,
Of sweetest thought, and happiest weal,
    With sense of purest toned delight;

And so this birthday, — thine and mine
    Is one unmeasured happiness;
And join I thus, my name with thine,
    That mine, thine may, by contact, bless.

If I see not thy face — nor hold
    Thy hand, with joy, in mine,
Yet I am with the thought consoled,
    That my birthday is also thine.

But yet I hope still, that e'er the gates,
    Swing in, upon their grating hinge,
And that grim messenger, who waits,
    And, to thee thy last summons brings,

To hide thee from the mortal sight,
    Of those who love thee, evermore,
In the damp rayless, death-dark, night,
    While moves the world on, as before.

Ere then, thy face I hope to see,
    If but a moment, that my hand
May clasp thine, then — the pledge to me,
    Of friendship, — truest strongest band.

And then the vision of thy face,
    Will strengthen me, and I'll remember
More in the heart's best, home-kept, place,
    THIS SEVENTEENTH DAY OF OUR DECEMBER.

The day shall, ever, thenceforth, come,
    Upon its yearly, time-fixed round,
Not as a mute, all voiceless, dumb,
    But chorused with full-chimed, glad sound

Of voices, mingling in the air,
    Singing in tones, most sweet to me,
On earth so unknown and so rare,
    The song of this, the meed to thee.

I'll bless thee for it, and may God
    Bless thee, and lead thee by the hand
With comfort, of His staff and rod,
    And bring thee to the border-land;

Then, gently, lay thee down to sleep,
    Closing thine eyes, for quiet rest,
While, well-appointed angels keep
    Thee, in thy sleep, secure and blest,

Until the last grand morn shall break,
    In beauty through the ambient skies;
Then mayst thou, all immortal wake,
    And in the Saviour's image rise.

I may work briefly for a while,
    Preaching wherever I may be,
With prayer, that Heaven may on me smile,
    And I some fruitage-good may see.

If I the Christ may, fully, preach,
    Him of Judea and Galilee;
And, in His name, the lowly reach,
    That they, his kindly face may see,

I will be satisfied, nor ask
    A higher honor — and, when done,
My pleasing, well-appointed task,
    It ending, with life's setting sun,

Then, I shall sleep, and I shall rise,
    When comes the morn of that glad day,
When, coming through the parting skies,
    The Christ will speed him on his way,

Back to the earth, he trod before,
    But not, as when he here, awhile,
The thorn-crown, ignominious, wore,
    When in Him, Pilate found no guile,

But, in His glory-bright, to reign;
    Fixing his throne where David's stood;
When earth shall bloom and smile again,
    And grows the Life Tree's, forest-wood.

Then may we sing amidst the throng,
    The multitude redeemed shall sing,
The glad Hosannas, rapturous song,
    As God shall His, to Zion bring.

Meanwhile, thou for the end, wilt wait
   In quiet peace, relieved of care;
Dear, precious friend, whom none can hate,
   Waiting amidst the gloaming there.

Now friend, adieu —*with God*— may He
   Bless thee, forever, through His Son;
By His own Spirit, all, the *three*,
   Until, at last, thy life is done,

Then thou shalt rest the *little while*,
   Until the morning-light shall dawn;
And, when all nature, in its smile,
   Shall answer, the salute of morn;

Then may we meet, where friends abide,
   Forever, without age or pain,
Where flows life's river's healing tide,
   Where Christ, The King of Earth, Shall Reign.

Yours for Christ
L. C. McKinstry

www.ingramcontent.com/pod-product-compliance
Lightning Source LLC
Chambersburg PA
CBHW020114170426
43199CB00009B/530